The GLORY OF ZION

Experience The Celestial Realm
While on Earth

CHARLES PAUL

Table of Content

THE POWER AT WORK IN YOU

TAKE ADVANTAGE OF THE POWER IN YOU

CHAPTER 4

ALL THINGS ARE YOURS

MANIFESTING THE GLORY

MYSTERY REVEALED

CHAPTER 5

GATES OF ZION

POWER FOR CHANGE.

CHAPTER 6

THE ZION LIFE

THE LOVE LIFE

INTRODUCTION

The Glory of Zion unveils the Kingdom of Christ in a world of uncertainty and turmoil. There exists a beacon of hope that transcends time and space. "The Glory of Zion" explains the kingdom of Christ and your position as a Christian. These pages unveil the timeless truths illuminating the glory and splendor of the Believer's dominion in Christ.

The kingdom of Christ is a testament to our Savior's infinite power and boundless love. It is a kingdom that surpasses the limitations of earthly realms. This book unlocks the mysteries surrounding this heavenly kingdom and your position in the kingdom.

This book presents a captivating exploration of the kingdom's manifold dimensions. From its inception in the ancient promises and prophecies to its establishment through the life, death, and resurrection of Jesus Christ and its ongoing expansion through the ministry of the Holy Spirit, we embark on an odyssey that uncovers the profound significance and relevance of this celestial realm in our daily lives.

It elucidates the values, principles, and transformative power of the kingdom of Christ, enabling us to embody its glory and usher in its reign here on Earth.

This book will empower you to embrace your role as a Citizen of the kingdom, inspiring you to live a victorious life.

Embark on this remarkable expedition into the glorious kingdom of Christ. May your heart be stirred, your spirit ignited, and your eyes unveiled as you discover who you are in Christ. "The Glory of Zion" is beckoning you to know that you are in Zion now, not when you die.

So, step into the pages before you and prepare to embark on a breathtaking adventure that will redefine your understanding of purpose, identity, and destiny in the kingdom of Christ. Welcome to "The Glory of Zion."

CHAPTER 1
Beautiful Zion

The LORD shall bless thee out of Zion: and thou shalt
see the good of Jerusalem all the days of thy life.

(Psa. 128:5 KJV)

One of the most important sites mentioned in the Bible is Zion. But it was more than just a location in the Old Testament. There are other implications, like the reign of our Lord Jesus Christ and His kingdom.

Zion is a vital and significant name in the Bible—the history, the life, and the kingdom of our Lord Jesus Christ. Zion was first referenced in the Bible in 2 Samuel 5:7.

Mount Zion

Initially, Zion was a real city on a hill outside Jerusalem's wall. The Temple of God was constructed on this mountain; Israel was also called Zion (Chosen people of God). The Old Testament's Mount Zion was a heavily fortified city that served as the location of God's chosen place of manifestation. It was a location where God's glory could be physically felt.

The LORD is great in Zion; and he is high above all the people. (Psa. 99:2 KJV)

Zion was more than just a real city with inhabitants. It served as God's base of operations on Earth. Zion was the location of God's temple, where one might encounter and witness God's grandeur. In Zion, God was present, and to experience God's glory, the nations flocked to Zion.

Spiritual Zion

In the New Testament, Zion alludes to the spiritual kingdom of God, where God's government is in charge.

Zion was a real location where people resided in the Old Testament. However, as you will later see in this book, the city of Zion served as a metaphor for God's plan and purpose with the new creation. Hallelujah! Christ is the realization of that plan.

When God first created Adam, he was given a kingdom that he later lost. In Christ, that throne and that power have been reinstated. Indeed, God desired a city where he alone would rule and reign and where His children would congregate. God has wanted this since creating Adam and placing him in the garden. As a result, Adam and God enjoyed communion in Eden.

Zion is a place of communion. It is a spiritual kingdom foretold in the prophecy regarding the arrival of Christ and His Kingdom.

> *In the last days the mountain of the LORD's house will be established as the highest of the mountains and raised above the hills. All the nations will stream to it. Then many people will come and say, "Let's go to the mountain of the LORD, to the house of the God of Jacob. He will teach us his ways so that we may live by them." The teachings will go out from Zion. The LORD's word will go out from Jerusalem.*
>
> *(Isa 2:2-3 GW)*

David conquered Zion and established the "City of God." Zion represents "the Kingdom of God," and Jesus promised it to those who believe in Him. Every believer anticipates the New Jerusalem that will descend from heaven. Rev 3:12, 21:2

Believers are already subject to the rule and influence of the kingdom of Christ while they are on Earth, even before the actual city of Jerusalem appears, where Christ will physically reign eternally.

Zion, The City of God

God's presence and splendor were physically present in Zion. Another significant characteristic of Zion was that it served as a stronghold and a refuge for the people of Israel. God made His presence known in Zion, God's physical dwelling place. It was a stronghold for the people of Israel because God was in their midst.

David was the one God used to cave out the city of Zion. He defeated the Jebusites and built the city of God, the same way Jesus defeated Satan and built a spiritual Zion, the city of God, the kingdom of God. Jesus came to establish a kingdom, a spiritual Zion, not a religion.

It is a city where God is paramount, and the Government of God is established. This is where we live now as Christians. When you said yes to Jesus, there was immediate transfiguration and translation; we have changed kingdom and are now in the kingdom of God's dear Son. We belong to God.

By default, every natural man has the nature of the devil. When you are born again, you are born into another kingdom and nature, the kingdom of God and our Lord Jesus, hallelujah! You are in His Kingdom now, not tomorrow, or when you transit into eternity. No! You are there now.

Open your spiritual eyes to see and understand the things that are yours by the Holy Spirit. Glory! As a citizen of the kingdom, an inheritance belongs to you that privileges you as a full citizen. Do you know about this? You cannot demand it if you do not know about it.

In this kingdom, you are a son, not a servant. Glory to Jesus! As a son, you have the same inheritance as Christ. In short, you are a Joint heir with Christ (Rom 8:17). What accrues to Jesus also accrues to you. The same love the Father has for Jesus is the same love the Father has for you (Col 1:12)

The same righteousness the Father gave to Jesus when He was born again (Rom. 8:29) is the same imputed to every believer. Therefore, Jesus does not have more righteousness than you.

Before Jesus went to the Cross, He was the only begotten son of God. After His resurrection, Jesus is no longer the only begotten son of God because God has many Children today, but Jesus is our elder brother, Lord, Savior, and all.

Christ's Rule on Earth

The spiritual Zion, also known as New Jerusalem, is the everlasting kingdom that Christ has established—the city where Christ will rule forever. Believers are living there now, hallelujah! Not tomorrow, not when we die; we are there now, glory!

Many believers are waiting to die before they can access this kingdom where the beauty of God is manifested in all things. No, you do not have to die before you can access the goodness of Zion. The kingdom of Zion is within you; take advantage of it.

The Physical new Jerusalem will come down from heaven, where Christ will rule forever. Yes, that is true. But as we are in this world, we are functioning from the realms of God; therefore, we are not ordinary.

We are supernatural beings. The physical new Jerusalem where Christ will rule forever will come from heaven; every Christian looks forward to this (Rev 21:2), but eternal life starts from here; you have it now, not in the new Jerusalem to come. Eternal life is the very life of God you received when you said yes to Jesus.

The difference is that now that you are in this body, eternal life is in your spirit, not your body, so there is a struggle to gain control between the spirit and the body. The more you mortify your body through the power of the Holy Ghost, the more eternal life manifests in your body and consequently affects your entire life.

But a day is coming when we shall put off this body either in death or on the resurrection (1Co 15:53-54). On that day, death shall be defeated, and we shall live in the fullness of our glorified bodies. Hallelujah! We shall put on immortality, and the body will no longer hinder us from living in the fullness of God.

The first Zion, with her glory, has passed away. This is the one David built for God, representing a place of worship for the people of Israel, where God manifested Himself in the Old Testament.

Jesus came and established the spiritual Zion, the city of the living God, which He built with His body on the cross and became the Author of eternal salvation (Heb. 5:9). Jesus is the gate by which any person will access the city of Zion.

The Mighty One, God, the LORD, speaks and summons the earth from the rising of the sun to where it sets. From Zion, perfect in beauty, God shines forth" (Psalm 50:1-2).

Anyone who accepts the life of God in his spirit becomes part of Zion. That is how to become a citizen of the kingdom of Zion. It is our place of refuge and communion with God. Hallelujah! Christ in you is the kingdom of God in you. You in Christ is your kingdom citizenship.

"By contrast, we have already come near to God in a totally different realm, the Zion-realm, for we have entered the city of

the Living God, which is the New Jerusalem in heaven! We have joined the festal gathering of myriads of angels in their joyous celebration! And as members of the church of the Firstborn all our names have been legally registered as citizens of heaven! And we have come before God who judges all, and who lives among the spirits of the righteous who have been made perfect in his eyes! And we have come to Jesus who established a new covenant with his blood sprinkled upon the mercy seat; blood that continues to speak from heaven, "forgiveness," a better message than Abel's blood that cries from the earth, "justice." (Heb. 12:22-24 TPT)

In Zion, believers are meant to have an intimate, sacred relationship with the Almighty. In this relationship, the fatherhood of God is revealed to the Kingdom's citizens. You will have an indebted revelational knowledge of the Father as He was, is, and will be.

While the Kingdom of Zion is real, Jesus is the point of reference from which the Kingdom of Zion is built in our hearts.

Today, believers have the inheritance and honor of living in Zion, the Kingdom of Heaven, or God's presence through the blood of Jesus that was shed on the cross of Calvary.

On the day of resurrection, the coming of our Lord Jesus with His Angels, we shall see Jesus in the eternal Zion. And in Zion, Believers shall live in His Holy presence forever.

CHAPTER 2

Heaven on Earth

"Then the LORD God formed the man from the dust of the earth and blew the breath of life into his nostrils. The man became a living being. The LORD God planted a garden in Eden, in the east. That's where he put the man whom he had formed."

(Gen 2:7-8 GW)

Beautiful Eden

After God finished creating Adam and Eve, God made a garden and put the man He created there, where He communed with Him daily. God created the whole earth but chose Eden as a meeting place with the man He made. When you look closely at the above verses, you will discover it was God who planted the garden and put the man there to enjoy the goodness of that garden. God is a good God. He knows what you need and is good for you; hallelujah!

The beauty of the garden was overwhelming. Four rivers supplied water to it (Gen2:10). Therefore, Eden would never dry. It would be evergreen all year round. It was from Eden that Adam could rule the whole earth; Eden symbolically means a place of rest, authority, and communion.

So, when Adam disobeyed, God sent Adam out of Eden to protect the Tree of Life in the garden so that Adam would not reach out and eat it and become irredeemable.

> *"After he sent the man out, God placed angels and a flaming sword that turned in all directions east of the Garden of Eden. He placed them there to guard the way to the tree of life."*
>
> *(Gen 3:24 GW)*

Adam lost these three things; rulership, authority, and communion. From then, the sons of Adam have been looking for a way to regain rulership, authority, and communion with God; this quest has led to the formation of various kinds of religion. Religion is never God's wisdom but man's idea to restore what he lost.

For Adam to effectively rule the earth with the authority given to him by God, there must be a place to meet with God, a place to wait on God. Eden was that place chosen by God. It was a place of strength, wisdom, and power; Eden was where God communed with Adam.

God's communion with Adam had spiritual and physical implications. Remember what happened to Moses after fellowshipping with God on the Mount for forty days and nights as he waited on God (Exo. 34:29-35). He was transfigured, his face shone, and the glory of God was literally upon Moses.

In the same way, Adam was full of God's glory because of God's manifest glory around his Physical body as he fellowshipped with God daily.

At the cool of the evening, God will come down and fellowship with Adam (Gen 3:8); through such intimacy, Adam received all that was required to govern the whole earth and all that God asked him to do. In the presence of God, Adam received daily strength, wisdom, and power(authority) to govern the whole earth; yes, all this was available through that evening's communion with God.

Without such intercourse, Adam could not have had such enablement to oversee the whole creation. God was his strength, wisdom, and power. Adam had authority, but all power belonged to God.

Though the whole earth belongs to God, He chose this special place called Aden to meet with the man Adam every evening.

All was going well with Adam, and the communion between Adam and God was maintained. Adam was operating in the class of God and could do all that God had created him to do; he was functioning in the capacity and class of God because he was the image of God.

Adam was living by revelation knowledge, not by the senses. Adam didn't need to go to school to learn about his environment. Adam knew everything by revelation, from the inside out. So, Earth was part of Heaven; things were done on Earth like in Heaven.

In Heaven, only God's word is settled. Heaven is Heaven because everyone obeys, speaks, and does the word of God, which is God's will. The Word of God is God *"In the beginning was the Word, and the Word was with God, and the Word was God." (Joh 1:1 KJV).*

The power of God is in His word. The power of his word holds everything together. (Heb. 1:3)

So, in Heaven, only the word of God is done. The word of God is also His will. Psalm 119:89 *"Forever the word of God is settled in Heaven."*

The will of God is perfect; perfection comes by following His word, which sustained Heaven. The beauty of Heaven is God's word; when the same word that made Heaven beautiful comes to settle in your life, when you embrace the word, He makes beauty out of you. Jesus is the Word made flesh; He is the living Word.

Three important things

> *"He hath made the earth by his power, he hath established the world by his wisdom, and hath stretched out the heaven by his understanding."(Jer. 51:15 KJV)*

There are three things God uses to create: His power, His wisdom, and His understanding. All these three things are talking about the same thing. The word of God is His power; it is God's wisdom as well as His understanding. All these three things speak of the greatness of God's word as the creator.

The word of God is light. Only God's will is done in Heaven. When Jesus began teaching His disciples how to pray, He told them they should pray. *"Thy will be done as it's done in heaven."* The will of God is done in Heaven, so there is peace and Joy in Heaven. Heaven's beauty is because God's will is perfect and Holy.

In Heaven, the Angels do not have their own will, you see! Their will is the word of God. Angels do not have blood like humans do. The natural human body is powered by blood; the word of God powers the Angels in Heaven, and the Angels move by the impulses of God's word. God is love, His will is love, and His word is love.

When the devil tried to establish his own will, the system of Heaven could not assimilate him. Because everything is held together in Heaven and Earth by the power of God's word, things would not have been the same if the devil had maintained his own will in Heaven.

Heaven would have become so chaotic like Earth today, but Satan was not allowed to do so; he was kicked out of Heaven, so he decided to try Earth, where God gave Adam authority, and Eve fell to the devil's deception.

God gave Adam the task of overseeing the Earth, never allowing Satan to establish his own will on Earth through his word. Will is exercised through words. Things have never been the same since the devil introduced his word on Earth through Eve. Obeying Satan's word has polluted creation and brought death and calamity to the Earth's inhabitants.

The word of God created the beautiful Earth in the beginning. Satan's word brought degeneration and destruction to the Earth God created and said, "It was beautiful" On our journey on Earth, it is all about words. Whose word do you obey? If you obey God's word, you are bringing Heaven to yourself.

Because Adam obeyed Satan's word, everything turned against him. Even the Animals God created for man to care for turned against Man. It was not so in the beginning. Adam had power over the Earth and its creation, but because Adam and Eve obeyed Satan's word and did his will, they lost that power to control because everything is held together by the power of God's word, not Satan's word.

New Jerusalem

Every believer looks forward to this great city of Zion because we all perceive it as a beautiful city built by God. The Bible talks about the floor made of Gold and the new Jerusalem coming down from Heaven. The beauty of this city is the beauty of God's word.

Today, the same word is in you in the person of Jesus Christ. Now the kingdom of God is in you; His glory is in you; His power is in you; and the beauty of Heaven is in you. Glory to God!

In Heaven, only the will of God is paramount. Now let me tell you why Heaven is such a beautiful place; it is because God's word, which is God's will, is what the heavenly beings live by.

For instance, God's word says "to love your neighbor" So, in Heaven, they obey, and everyone loves and cares; you see why Heaven is peaceful. While on Earth, people do what pleases them. Politicians and governments do their will, leading to poverty, war, and starvation.

That is why the Earth is in such a chaotic and turbulent condition, with wars everywhere. If the Government and Leaders of nations had obeyed the word of God that says to love and forgive one another, all the wars that were fought in the past would not have been fought.

You see! Immediately Adam and His descendant refused to keep the word of God that held everything together; everything degenerated.

Now in Zion, the very beauty of God that Adam rejected is in your heart; speak it forth through your mouth to bring the beauty and glory of Zion into physical manifestation.

Jesus taught His Apostles how to walk in the glory of Zion while on this planet Earth; He said, "Let your will be done on earth as it's done in heaven." This prayer of Jesus reveals the secret of the beauty of Heaven.

You can bring Heaven into your life, oh yes! If the word of God is what made Heaven beautiful, if you do the word of God and allow it to dwell in you richly, it will bring the beauty of Heaven into you.

Any time you are doing God's word, you are doing His will; the word of God is the glory of Heaven. Therefore, you can be on Earth and live a life of Heaven. Whether in your marriage or finances, you can live victoriously as though in Heaven while on Earth.

The Creative force

The word of God has creative force. It can produce what it says; in the beginning, the Earth was without form, and empty darkness was upon the face of the deep.

> *"In the beginning God created the heaven and the earth. And the earth was without form, and void; and darkness was upon the face of the deep. And the Spirit of God moved upon the face of the waters. And God said, Let there be light: and there was light."*
>
> *(Gen 1:1-3 KJV)*

This refers to an abject condition. Nevertheless, this passage demonstrates the efficacy of God's Word. The creative force of God's Word, God said, "Let there be light" Immediately, there was light. The Word of God is light, producing all the beautiful things you see around you today.

The same Word, if allowed in, will quicken and bring healing to your mortal body. It will restore whatever you have lost and make your life beautiful. Hallelujah!

The devil knows the importance of God's Word. He is after the Word and goes after the Word in your spirit. If he can take the Word away from you, he has taken your Heaven away. He has taken away the involvement of God in your life because God gets involved in you through his Word.

The Word of God in you is Heaven in you. God gets involved in people's lives through His Word; when the people of Israel needed healing, God sent His Word and healed them. When He wanted to save the world, God sent His Word to the world; His Word became flesh and dwelt amongst us (John 1:14).

Satan was in Heaven before being banished, so he understood the rules. All Satan wanted was to make Adam go against the Word of God.

Satan knew the consequences because he tried it and lost his position in Heaven, so to get Adam kicked out and take over his authority,

Satan needed to deceive Adam and Eve into going against the Word of God, which God warned them from the beginning to guard the earth against the intruder the devil. *And the LORD God took the man and put him into the garden of Eden to dress it and to keep(Guard)it. (Gen 2:15 KJV)*

> *The Bible says, "Know ye not, that to whom ye yield yourselves servants to obey, his servants ye are to whom ye obey; whether of sin unto death, or of obedience unto righteousness?"*
>
> *(Rom 6:16 KJV).*

When Adam rejected God's word and obeyed Satan's word, Adam became a servant to Satan, and Satan became his boss *"to whom ye yield yourselves servants to obey, his servants ye are to whom ye obey."*

All Satan wanted was to make Adam go against the Word. He needed to get Adam to disobey the Word of God and not to do God's will, and immediately Satan lured Adam into disobeying God through Eve, his wife; he died, divinity left him, and Adam was sent out of Eden.

Heaven in You

When the Word of God was in place in Adam's life, Adam enjoyed Heaven on Earth. Heaven left him the moment he rebelled against the very word that made heaven beautiful. At that moment, beauty left his life, toiling, sweat, and thorns became part of Adam's life.

The Word of God is the Power, Wisdom, and glory of the kingdom of God. Therefore, anytime a child of God is defeated by the circumstances of life, watch out if he has forsaken the Word.

What the devil is after is the Word. To squeeze the Word out of your life, the Word of God is Heaven in you. So, Eden was a place of fellowship, not just a location. It symbolized authority and a meeting point with God and Adam.

Since Eden and the entire Earth were to be an extension of Heaven, the will of God must be carried out in all things as in Heaven.

God gave Adam authority to govern the earth, but that authority was in God, and God was in Adam, you see! Adam's authority was not outside of God. This means that authority was functional and Effective if Adam obeyed and communed with God.

Adam could not function under that authority outside of God. When Adam disobeyed, he lost that authority to the devil. As a believer, in the same way, God has given you authority over the enemy's powers; that authority is not outside of God; that authority is Christ, and Christ is in you. Christ in you is Heaven in you.

Christ is the hope of the glory of that authority. That is why those outside Christ cannot access it. When Adam departed from God's Word, he lost the heavenly and became ordinary. Adam fell from the class where he was created and became something lower; to an extent, he could not stand God's presence, which he used to before he disobeyed.

Adam was sent away from the presence of God; there is no vacuum in the realm of the spirit. There is no sitting on the fence. We have God and his kingdom. Unfortunately, we also have the devil and his cohorts. Anyone who has received the life Of Jesus has been translated into the kingdom of God's dear Son.

Immediately Adam disobeyed; he crossed the kingdom and became the child of the devil; Adam lost the power of his Word. Before then, Adam's Word was as powerful as God's. The story of redemption is the plan of God to restore man. From that moment on, Adam's life became full of sweat and thorns.

The Power of Words

In Christ, we have been restored to that Authority Adam lost in the garden; we are no longer ordinary we have been recreated and given a new nature. The power of our word has been restored; we can say a thing, and it will come to pass.

In Zion, your words are spirit and life. You participate in this unseen kingdom through words; your Word is you and your representative. Therefore, whatever you say is what you affirm.

You can build Heaven around you with words; the Word of God is settled in Heaven. So, settle the same Word in your life; it will build Heaven in your marriage, finance, health, etc.

By doing the will of God in your marriage, you can only expect Heaven. Remember, prosperity and Marriage is God's idea; it was not a man who initiated it. So, what is God saying concerning marriage, finances, health, etc.? Whatever God is saying, that is His will. You will succeed in these things if you apply God's will.

I have said it numerous times. To succeed, you must carefully adhere to and do what God says concerning that area of life.

The world has its model and understanding of every aspect of life, that is, human wisdom, but that wisdom is limited; it is still searching for solutions for many things. I am not saying it does not solve any problem! That is not what I am insinuating; I am simply saying that man's wisdom is limited and cannot solve all the problems of Man.

The wisdom of God has no limitations. It has been tested, and it can work anywhere, anytime. There is something wrong in Christendom today; even the church teaches man's wisdom and has rejected God's wisdom and counsel concerning every aspect of life.

For God intended that your faith not be established on man's wisdom but by trusting in his almighty power. (1Co 2:5 TPT)

The world's model has limitations. It is a trial-and-error kind; sometimes, it works, and other times it doesn't. Because of this, believers are getting the same result as the rest of the world. Bring Heaven into your endeavors; it is possible; that is what God wants.

Let the people of this world see Heaven in you. When you remove God's Word, I assure you that God is not there. You are doing your own thing. The wisdom of man is limited. Such wisdom will ground one's life. Such wisdom will start a race without finishing it.

God and His Word are one; wherever His Word is, God is present. "He sent his Word and healed their diseases" God does not need to be there physically. When you run your business with God's Word, God is there. Whatever you are doing outside God's Word is outside of God.

Adam was given authority to oversee the earth, but that authority was in God. If Adam's intimacy and communion with God were not altered, that authority remained, and that authority was functional if Adam was operating according to God's will; as soon as he stepped away from God's will, he stepped away from that authority, God gave him.

The authority God gave Adam was not outside God but in God, which means Adam had to maintain a steady communion with God for that authority to be relevant. That authority was God in Adam; the day he lost God, he lost that authority.

That authority has been restored to everyone in Zion; in Christ, we have been fully restored, hallelujah.

CHAPTER 3
The Power at Work in You

"I pray that the light of God will illuminate the eyes of your imagination, flooding you with light, until you experience the full revelation of the hope of his calling—that is, the wealth of God's glorious inheritances that he finds in us, his holy ones! I pray that you will continually experience the immeasurable greatness of God's power made available to you through faith. Then your lives will be an advertisement of this immense power as it works through you! **This is the mighty power that was released when God raised Christ from the dead** *and exalted him to the place of highest honor and supreme authority in the heavenly realm!*

(Eph 1:18-20 TPT)

P aul was praying for the people of Ephesus that the light of God would illuminate their eyes. This prayer should be prayed in churches today. The Holy Spirit inspired this prayer.

Believers' eyes must be flooded with light until they experience the full revelation of their hope in Christ. Many believers live their lives as though there is no hope in which God called us, but it should not be so. There is an abundant wealth of God's glorious inheritance for us who believe in Christ.

The immeasurable greatness of God's power works in us who believe in Christ; hallelujah! This power is available to you through the same Spirit that raised Christ from death.

Take Advantage of The Power in You

Many Zion dwellers are unaware of the exceeding greatness of God's power working in them; the Bible says the same power that raised Christ from death is at work in every believer.

I pray that God will open your eyes to see his light so that you can see the hope he has called you, the abundance of the magnificent blessings he offers His people, and the immeasurable power working in those of us who believe.

This power at work in us is the same strength God employed to raise Christ from the dead and place him on His right side in the celestial realm.

Glory to God! There is unlimited greatness of God's power, working mightily to produce strength for the believer. This power is the same power God operated in Christ when he brought him back to life.

Paul was inspired to write to the church about this great power we carry inside. Imagine you are carrying the power that raised Christ from the dead, and your body is still sick; that is an error.

You must know who you are in Christ and who Christ is in you; adequate and full knowledge of what Christ has done will communicate and impact divinity in your body. It will cause you to function in higher realms of glory.

The devil does not want the eyes of your understanding to be flooded with the light of God's word; he wants you to be in the dark as far as the work of the cross is concerned so that he will whip you hard.

Satan is okay with you becoming a nominal Christian without adequate information about what Christ has done for you.

You need to know what and who you are in Christ, for Christ has become your wisdom, righteousness, and redemption. *"My people are destroyed for lack of knowledge: because thou hast rejected knowledge" (Hos. 4:6 KJV)*

I traveled to Nairobi, Kenya, for mission work. While driving around, I mistakenly failed their traffic rule because I was using GPS to navigate the city, so the GPS gave me the wrong direction.

The traffic police saw me and pursued me with a Police bike; he flagged me down. Though the Policeman knew it was an unintentional misdirection from GPS, he still booked me, and I paid the fine, you see! Ignorance is not an excuse.

In the realm of the spirit, the same is applicable; ignorance has consequences, and most Christians suffer today because of ignorance. If you knowingly or unknowingly jump from a twenty-story building, the law of gravity will take effect.

Lack and poverty among believers today result from knowingly or unknowingly going against spiritual laws concerning finances.

Take time to learn about spiritual laws. Tell the Holy Ghost to draw your attention to these spiritual truths. That was exactly what Paul was praying for the early Church: The Eyes of the Church would be flooded with light so that they could see and obey these spiritual truths without violating them.

Whenever the church is mentioned, people will look at the building called the church without knowing that they are the church as an individual. So, this power belongs to us individually and collectively. God has called you into a glorious life as an individual and collectively as a church.

Are you living the glorious life God promised us in the Bible concerning his son? Are you lost and nowhere to be found? Guard your loins and stand up again. Let the word walk ahead of you, and be light on your path; it will disperse darkness and lead you into your inheritance.

CHAPTER 4
All things Are Yours

God's divine power has given us everything we need for life and for godliness. This power was given to us through knowledge of the one who called us by his own glory and integrity. Through his glory and integrity he has given us promises of the highest value. Through these promises you will share in the divine nature because you have escaped the corruption that sinful desires cause in the world.

(2Pe 1:3-4 GW)

Zion is a life of glory; anything short of this is unacceptable. If your life does not manifest the glory of Christ, do not take it; if you are not living gloriously, do not just cover it with religion. Find out why because His divine power has given you everything you need for life and godliness. Go into intense prayer, and find out the will of

God through prayer by cooperating with His *word. You can refer to my book (Charles Paul: God Answers Prayer)*

God never lies if His word says, *"His divine power has given you everything you need for life and godliness"* Then find out why things are not the way they should be in your life.

Jabez did the same in Bible (1Ch 4:9 – 10). Jabez was a person of honor. He was more respected than his brothers, and everyone looked up to him, but things were not working out for Jabez as they should.

His mother had named him Jabez [sorrow] because his birth was painful, so all the days of Jabez were sorrows and pains. One day, he decided to change things through prayer; Jabez prayed, "Oh Lord, that You would truly bless me and enlarge my border, that You would be with me, and that You would keep evil at bay so that it wouldn't grieve me." Jabez prayed, and God granted him his request.

You see! Do not just take anything that life brings to you and wish in your heart that one day it will change; it may never change until something is done or you do something about it. You need to take what belongs to you forcefully, take back your marriage, health, and finances. Take back whatever the enemy has stolen from you. *"From the time of John, the Baptizer until now, the kingdom of heaven has been forcefully advancing, and forceful people have been seizing it." (Mat 11:12 GW)*

So, if you are not manifesting the glory of Jesus, do not heap the blames on God; everything needed to be done on God's part; God has done them. He has provided it in Christ, and Christ died once and for all. He is not going to die again. Check the receiving side because the source is always okay. God has called you to a life of progress, success, and glory.

God appeared unto Abraham in Mesopotamia before he came to live in Charran (Act 7:2). Before God appeared to Abraham, there was nothing glorious about this man Abraham. Everything about Abraham was nothing to write about until the Father of Glory revealed himself to Abraham in Genesis 14. The Father of Glory has revealed himself to the world in the person of His son Jesus Christ. He is the totality of God manifest in human form, according to Col. 2:9;

*"**The Son is the dazzling radiance of God's splendor, the exact expression of God's true nature**—his mirror image! He holds the*

universe together and expands it by the mighty power of his spoken word"... (Heb. 1:3 TPT)

Abraham encountered God in Genesis 14; on the next page, Abraham was rich in Silver and Gold. You cannot be with the father of glory, and your life is not glorious; how? God is the Father of glory; the Father shares His glory with them in Zion; praise God forevermore!

Onesimus was a servant to Philemon. This guy was a con man. He scammed his master, Philemon, and ran away with his money. While Onesimus was running away with his master's fortune, he encountered Paul the Apostle, a man carrying God's glory. From that moment on, Onesimus' life became beautiful and glorious.

Paul impacted him with the beauty of Jesus and became his spiritual father. Onesimus was Once tagged as a useless and unprofitable servant, but when he met Paul, he became useful both for the ministry and his master, whom he stole from (Philemon 1:10–11).

History has it that this Onesimus, who was tagged useless, later became the Bishop of Ephesus. If your life is not in line with what it should be, find people who, through knowledge and faith in Christ, have become acquainted with the glory of heaven; follow them and learn the principles, and your life will become glorious too.

People say God does not share His glory with anyone, but that is untrue. If God does not share His glory with you, then there will be no glory in your life because he is the source of glory.

"And the glory which thou gavest me I have given them; that they may be one, even as we are one:" (Joh 17:22 KJV)

" We have become his poetry, a re-created people that will fulfill the destiny he has given each of us, for we are joined to Jesus, the Anointed One. Even before we were born, God planned in advance our destiny and the good works we would do to fulfill it!" (Eph. 2:10 TPT)

You are God's masterpiece, His poetry; you know what that means. You reflect everything God is: His Wisdom, righteousness, power, and Glory. Whatever made Him beautiful, you perfectly reflect all of them.

God recreated you to experience and reflect His glory, yes! Truly, you were made for His purpose.

It does not matter what you are going through; remember that you are the beauty of His creation, a perfect reflection of His wisdom, power, and righteousness. If you have received Christ, you are destined for a glorious life. So, it is time to walk into this glorious life that the Father has shared with us in Christ.

Refuse to allow your experience or what people say to define your direction; let God's word do that, looking unto Jesus, the author and the finisher of your faith (Heb. 12:2).

Looking unto Jesus means refusing to look at what the economist is saying; do not look at what the doctor is saying. If you continue looking at the economic data or what the doctor has said, you will go down. Set your gaze on Jesus, look unto Him, and live.

Without being distracted, set your heart on him, *"who can do exceedingly abundantly above all that you ask or think, according to the power that is working in you."* Eph 3:20

Never doubt God's mighty power to work in you and accomplish all this. He will achieve infinitely more than your greatest request, your most unbelievable dream, and exceed your wildest imagination! He will outdo them all, for his miraculous power constantly energizes you. (Eph. 3:20 TPT)

The Glory of God in you is what will put you over in life. Do not be discouraged; know this: things are working for your Good (Rom. 8:26); you are more than a conqueror in all these things.

There is the glory available for those in Christ Jesus now, not in the sweet by and by, so desire it more, and by knowledge, you will lay hold of the things freely given to you by the Spirit of God.

Manifesting The Glory

I have said, Ye are gods, and all of you are children of the most High. But ye shall die like men and fall like one of the princes. (Psa. 82:6-7 KJV)

God is the source of Glory, and the Father of Glory Ephesians 1:17. The Bible has revealed that we are gods; you read such scripture with the utmost attention and meditate on it until it becomes a reality. Do not shy away from such scriptures.

Many believers shy away from such scriptures because of their religious mindset. Seeing themselves in the class of God makes them feel they are dishonoring God; no, you are not! The Bible says you are in the class of God; that is exactly who you are.

Before Adam committed treason, he was in the class of God; whatever he said came to pass. Adam used the words of his mouth to rule the world; there was power in Adam's words. By his word, he named all the animals, whatever he called each of them, and they became Gen 2:19, so a lion is that way because Adam called it a Lion, and immediately it became "Lionic."

Adam was the image of God and the son of God; everything produces its kind. God produced His kind in Adam. That was why he could discuss and fellowship with God in the cool of the evening.

I was watching a documentary on how different animals interact and communicate within themselves when I learned that elephants could only understand and communicate within themselves only, just as lions or any other animal can interact with themselves alone. For God to communicate with you means you are made in the Class of God in Christ. Adam lost it, and Jesus restored it.

When Adam sinned, he fell out of that class and into a lower class that could no longer hold discussions and fellowship with God. Jesus came to set the man back from where he fell.

"For whatsoever things were written aforetime were written for our learning, that we through patience and comfort of the scriptures might have hope." (Rom 15:4 KJV)

This Bible verse identifying us as gods is for our learning. It is for us to know who we are; you cannot operate beyond the knowledge you have about yourself. Some Christians still see themselves as good-for-nothing lost sinners trying to beg and find favor from God, a million times no!

The death of Christ on the cross was an event that changed the cause of our lives; it was the event that moved us back to the position Adam was in before the fall; anyone who believes in Christ is restored to sonship. *"But as many as received him, to them gave he power to*

become the sons of God, even to them that believe on his name:"
(Joh. 1:12 KJV)

Many believers are merely existing, not knowing who they are in Christ; they go to church, sing Hymns, and never know their placement in God. We are raised with Christ, and now we sit together in the heavenly realms in Christ Jesus, over and beyond every name mentioned—both in the present world and the one to come, above principality and powers.

If you do not know who you are in Christ, you may classify yourself as ordinary. You are not ordinary—the greater one lives in you. God's children are in the same class as their Father God; you are not ordinary; you carry the DNA of your Father God, and you are God's child. Therefore, you ought to manifest His glory.

Jesus also quoted the same scripture, *"The Jewish leaders responded,*
"We're not stoning you for anything good you did, it's because
of your blasphemy! You're just a son of Adam, but you've claimed to
be God!" Jesus answered, "Isn't it written in your Scriptures that
God said, 'You are gods?' The Scriptures cannot be denied or found
to be in error."(Joh. 10:33-34 TPT)

Some still struggle to understand why the Bible fully refers to them as gods. You act more fully in your divine essence the more you recognize and accept divine truths.

You find it difficult to relate to the Bible's idea that you are in the class of God when you consider your life and everything you are currently experiencing, right?

Perhaps the question that pops into your head is this: if I belong to God's class, why aren't things working out for me? I suppose this information is being revealed so that you might accept it and enter the grandeur God has planned for you.

Do you realize God has chosen you to reveal His Glory in this generation? Oh yes!

"But you are God's chosen treasure—priests who are kings, a spiritual "nation" set apart as God's devoted ones. He called you out of darkness to experience his marvelous light, and now he claims you as his very own. He did this so that you would broadcast his glorious wonders throughout the world." (1Pe 2:9 TPT)

Everything that God accomplished was done so that You may share His beautiful wonders with the entire world. God created you for this reason—so that wherever you go, people can see the splendor of His presence that distinguishes you from the rest of the world.

During Paul's sermon in Lystra (Act 14:8–15), there was a lame man who had never walked and was crippled. He watched as Paul spoke as he sat there.

When Paul observed that the man had faith, he turned to him and said, "You! In the mighty name of our Savior Jesus, rise to your feet. The man immediately leaped to his feet, stood up, and began walking.

The masses exclaimed in their Lycaonian language, *"The gods have become like men and have come down to us!"* after witnessing what Paul had accomplished. That is exactly what it is; hallelujah! We are gods. This is how we display God's glory and attributes everywhere we go.

The Zeus priest brought bulls and flowers when he learned what had happened. Acts 14:13 states that he and the people wanted to offer sacrifice for the Apostles. Paul said, "We are humans like you but with divinity at work in us."

Mystery Revealed

> *Even the mystery which hath been hid from ages and*
> *from generations, but now is made manifest to his*
> *saints: (Col 1:26)*

Did you notice that everything under the sun has its appointed time? God withheld the splendor He revealed in Christ for ages and generations. Christ in you is the revelation of that secret, the grandeur He has shown us today.

God has chosen to make this mystery known in our days. How fortunate we are to be of the generation to witness God's Glory revealed in our oneness with Christ! This glory is yours now. People yearned to enter this Glory in the Old Testament but were not permitted to do so because it was not for them. Romans 16:25 -26.

Through the gospel, eternity has been brought to light. This wonderful good news is the unveiling of the mystery kept secret from the beginning of creation until now. The prophets longed for it, spoke about it, and observed it from a distance, but they did not enter since it was not intended for them. The fact that Christ has moved into you is the glory and secret revealed.

It is sad to observe that most Christians have no idea who they are; they barely survive in the hope that they will one day meet the Lord when they pass away. Of course, believers will see Jesus in sweet by and by, but now you are on earth; you are an Ambassador of Zion. Do not wait until you die before you walk in the glory, oh no! Christ in you now is that glory, so the glory is present and will continue in the future.

Most believers hope in the beautiful hereafter, so they manage to get by in life with broken hearts, legs, and heads; they are barely living, hoping that one day when they die, they will meet the lord; of course, that is true, yet the eternal life you desperately desire begins now.

The body and the spirit conflict because Eternal life exists in the spirit; as you mortify the body and its wants, eternal life will flow from your spirit and manifest in your physical body. No restrictions will be left once you remove this earthly suit in death, then believers will live in their glorified bodies with the Lord Jesus,

Here on Earth, eternal life begins. Those in Zion do not have the same life as those outside Zion; those in the kingdom of Zion have the nature and life of God in them, hallelujah! None of us are ordinary. We have passed from death to life, John 5:25. The life in you is not in the blood. You are supernatural;

But as many as received him, to them gave he the power to become the sons of God, even to them that believe on his name: Which were born, not of blood, nor of the will of the flesh, nor of the will of man, but of God. (Joh 1:12-13 KJV)

Because no one takes advantage of what they do not know, many believers are defeated because they do not know they have the God kind of life.

When you say yes to Jesus, you receive eternal life, which begins here. Immediately, righteousness is imputed to you.

> *He that believeth on the Son of God hath the witness in himself: he that believeth not God hath made him a liar; because he believeth not the record that God gave*

of his Son. And this is the record, that God hath given to us eternal life, and this life is in his Son. He that hath the Son hath life; and he that hath not the Son of God hath not life.

(1Jn 5:10-12 KJV)

Many believe Zion is a spiritual kingdom, so one can only enter it after death. Can I shock you, if you have received the testimony of God about His Son Jesus, you are in Zion, though it is a spiritual kingdom. You are a member of God's kingdom while still in this body.

" But we are a colony of heaven on earth as we cling tightly to our life-giver, the Lord Jesus Christ" (Php 3:20 TPT).

Did you see that? We are a colony of heaven on earth! That means our citizenship is in heaven, so stop trying to become like the people of this world. Stop imitating the ideas and opinions of the world's culture but be completely transformed and reformed by renewing your mind.

You have been raised with Christ; you should yearn for everything up there where Christ is seated at the seat of all power, dignity, and authority.

Yes, indulge in all the heavenly realm's riches and let heavenly truths, not earthly distractions, dominate your thoughts. Your crucifixion with Christ severed your connection from the world, and as a result, Christ has become the hiding place of your actual self. Hallelujah!

You begin to lay hold of your possessions more firmly the instant you realize that you are a part of God's kingdom now, not someday in the sweet by and by.

You are a full citizen with all the rights and privileges of the kingdom. We are operating from a different realm in this world. Even though you live in this world, you are not of it; you are a member of a spiritual kingdom where Christ is king. Our place of residence is in Zion. Philippians 3:20

" I have given them thy word, and the world hath hated them, because ***they are not of the world, even as I am not of the world****. I pray not that thou shouldest* ***take them out of the world****, but that thou*

*shouldest keep them from the evil. **They are not of the world, even as I am not of the world.** Sanctify them through thy truth: thy word is truth. **As thou hast sent me into the world, even so have I also sent them into the world.** " (Joh. 17:14-18 KJV)*

Even though you are not of this world, you have been given a mission to carry out on earth with the support of the powers of heaven. You serve as God's Agent; the complete might of heaven is behind you as you move around. You may appear to be average to others, yet you are not.

Every believer needs to be aware of their true nature. The power behind you is what differentiates you. Do you realize that there is power behind you? Do you know about it?

A lion growing up around sheep will believe it is a sheep until it realizes it is a lion. At that point, it starts acting like a lion by going on hunts and not depending on the daily ration provided to the sheep.

The lion immediately realizes its actual nature; it was born naturally "Lionic" without learning it.

You, therefore, belong to God; as a citizen of heaven rather than a candidate for it, you should base your actions on His kingdom; Don't operate inside the framework of this world; it has a different system from the one you came from.

Jesus reminded Himself that He is not of this world; you must constantly remind yourself of where you came from. The laws of this world do not restrict you; you are supernatural.

Believers live in this world physically; we attend the same schools and shop at the same supermarkets as everyone else, but our moral standards are different. You should distinguish yourself and fix your attention on those things that are above where Christ is seated.

The spiritual city of Zion is where every believer is now, it will continue after death, but it starts here on earth; you start experiencing the Zion life now, and the Zion life is living in the supernatural.

If we receive the witness of men, the witness of God is greater: for this is the witness of God which he hath testified of his Son. He that believeth on the Son of God hath the witness in himself: he that believeth not God hath made him a liar; because he believeth not the record that God gave of his Son. ***And this is the record, that God hath given to us eternal life, and this life is in his Son. He that hath the Son hath life; and he that hath not the Son of God hath not life.*** *These things have I written unto you that believe on the name of the Son of God;* ***that ye may know that ye have eternal life, and that ye may believe on the name of the Son of God.*** *(1Jn 5:9-13 KJV)*

You have eternal life now; God will not give it to you when you die! You have it now. God has already given it to you. Eternal life is God's kind of life.

It is derived from the Greek word "Zoe." However, the English language does not have a better word to translate it, so translators use the word eternal life, which means to live forever in the English language; going with the Greek meaning, it is more than just living forever because even Satan will live forever, and that does not mean he has eternal life.

I hope you know both the wicked and the righteous shall leave forever. It all depends on where, whether in hell or the New Jerusalem, the Physical city of Zion prepared by God.

At the end of this age, God will bring physical Zion down from heaven—the new Jerusalem. If you have eternal life now, you are part of this kingdom (Rev. 21:2).

The Bible signifies that you are in this world and not of this world. Eternal life in you makes you superhuman; yes, you are now in God's class.

The more you meditate and believe the word of God, the more these things become real to you. These truths are more than human wisdom can comprehend.

I was teaching at a Bible school in Johannesburg, South Africa. I brought up the topic of the new creation realities. I taught them about eternal life; I told them we have it now, not after we die, but now while in this physical body.

One of the students could not believe it. I tried to get him to believe it, but he could not. I asked him, "Do you believe the Bible? He said, "Yes," I asked him, "If it is in the Bible?" He said, "Yes," then do you believe it? He said, "No."

The truth scattered his religious theology. That is what truth does—it beats you into shape. Everything that young man believed for years was brought down under the light of God's word. He made an excuse to go out to cool off his brain, and I allowed him to go cool off his brain.

That brother tried to believe with his mental faculties, not from his heart. That has been the problem for many Believers today: believing with their heads. The truth of God's word cannot be grasped with your thinking faculty but only through meditation and confession until it becomes an established truth in your heart (spirit)

Unless it gets into your heart, it will not stick; this is the same problem why people cannot grasp the teaching of the Trinity, Jesus being God, and Mary conceived without a man but by the power of the Holy Ghost.

*Your hearts can soar with joyful gratitude when you think of how **God made you worthy to receive the glorious inheritance freely given to us by living in the light.** He has **rescued us completely from the tyrannical rule of darkness and has translated us into the kingdom realm of his beloved Son.** (Col 1:12-13 TPT)*

Hallelujah, He has already translated us. It will not happen in the future; this has already happened. If this has occurred, you are already in the kingdom if you have said yes to Jesus.

It is possible to be in this kingdom realm and never get the inheritances due to a lack of knowledge. Many do not know they are in Zion now; this has been the major problem for believers; they are waiting to be part of this kingdom after they have died, therefore not taking advantage of their inheritance in Christ now.

The word "translated" is the Greek word "metatithēmi" It means to transfer, so we have been transferred to Zion.

The same word "translated" was used when the Bible recorded how God took Enoch without seeing death. The Bible records that he was translated into heaven, just as you were translated into the kingdom of God's dear Son when you said yes to Jesus, you immediately changed location. All these things happen in the realm of the spirit while you are in the physical realm.

This has given us a great advantage in operating both in this world and the realm of the spirit, so we are masters of all circumstances. We can use the wisdom of men. When it does not bring answers, we switch to the wisdom of God.

As citizens of Zion, we have an advantage over those who are not. Paul and Silas were in prison, they must have explained to the authorities, but they would not let them go, so they switched to the wisdom of God and got it fixed; glory to God!

The kingdom of God is a real kingdom; though it is unseen does not mean it does not exist. It does exist. The Bible spoke about two kingdoms in Col 1;12, the kingdom of darkness and the kingdom of God's Son, Jesus Christ.

CHAPTER 5

Gates of Zion

"Moses stood in the camp gate and said, who is on the LORD'S side? Let him come unto me. And all the sons of Levi gathered themselves together unto him."

(Exo 32:26).

The physical Zion located in Jerusalem had gates through which people went into it and accessed the glory of God. These gates symbolize what Christ has done for us and what He is still doing today through the Holy Ghost.

Throughout the scriptures, we find Gates to be a gathering place for decision-making. Two angels met Lot as he sat at the gate of Sodom (Gen 19:1). A gate signifies authority and power; decisions are made at the gate.

Moses stood at a place of authority; A decision taken at the Gate was binding on the people. Elders gathered at the city Gate to make judgments and important decisions for the entire city, binding on the people.

Elders are those the king of the universe has put His Glory on. They think and do the will of the king; the Elders are the king's representatives; they Judge according to the king's will, and their judgment is the king's.

In Zion, you have been given authority to make decisions on behalf of the king; whatever you bind on earth, the same shall be bound in heaven (Matthew 16:19,18:18). You have been given power of attorney to use the name of Jesus to effect changes.

"If a man has a stubborn and rebellious son, which will not obey the voice of his father, or the voice of his mother, and that when they have chastened him, will not hearken unto them: ***Then shall his father and his mother lay hold on him, and bring him out unto the elders of his city, and unto the gate of his place;*** *And they shall say unto the elders of his city, This our son is stubborn and rebellious, he will not obey our voice; he is a glutton, and a drunkard. And all the men of his city*

shall stone him with stones, that he die: so shalt thou put evil away from among you; and all Israel shall hear, and fear." (Deu. 21:18-21) KJV

If any man takes a wife, and go in unto her, and hate her, And give occasions of speech against her, and bring up an evil name upon her, and say, I took this woman, and when I came to her, I found her not a maid: **Then shall the father of the damsel, and her mother, take and bring forth the tokens of the damsel's virginity unto the elders of the city in the gate: And the damsel's father shall say unto the elders***, I gave my daughter unto this man to wife, and he hateth her; And, lo, he hath given occasions of speech against her, saying, I found not thy daughter a maid; and yet these are the tokens of my daughter's virginity. And they shall spread the cloth before the elders of the city. And the elders of that city shall take that man and chastise him; And they shall amerce him in a hundred shekels of silver, and give them unto the father of the damsel because he hath brought up an evil name upon a virgin of Israel: and she shall be his wife; he may not put her away all his days. (Deu 22:13-19) KJV*

And if the man like not to take his brother's wife, then let his **brother's wife go up to the gate unto the elders***, and say, My husband's brother* *refuseth to raise up unto his brother a name in Israel, he will not perform the duty of my husband's brother. (Deu 25:7 KJV)*

In the Bible days, important decisions were made at the Gate. The elders assembled to make decisions at the Gate of the city; the authority of The Gate is the authority of the church today. Gates were so important and strategic that, in the days of war, the main target was to take hold of the enemy's Gate.

That is why the church of Jesus Christ is the target of satanic attacks through deception, blackmail, false teachers, and prophets. Jesus gave us His word, and the words of Jesus have become the spirit of prophecy.

> *"And I say also unto thee, That thou art Peter, and upon this rock I will build my church; **and the gates of hell shall not prevail against it."***

> *(Mat 16:18)*

Because Gates were strategically important, an entire city would surrender if an enemy captured its Gate during wars. In times of conflict, cities station their greatest army and fortress at the Gate, making it the most closely defended location.

If you have power over the gate of your adversary, you also have control over the entire city. When God blessed Abraham, one of the things God told him was that his seed would possess the Gate of his foes.

> *"And said, By myself have I sworn, saith the LORD, for because thou hast done this thing, and hast not withheld thy son, thine only son: That in blessing I will bless thee, and in multiplying I will multiply thy seed as the stars of the heaven, and as the sand which is upon the sea shore, **and thy seed shall possess the gate of his enemies;"***
>
> *(Gen 22:16-17) KJV.*

*"And I say also unto thee, That thou art Peter, and upon this rock I will build my church**; and the gates of hell** shall not prevail against it. (Mat 16:18)." KJV.* The kingdom of Satan also has Gates, which speak of the demonic powers. These powers have been unleashed against the body of Christ, but the power emanating from the Gate of

Zion is greater than that of the kingdom of darkness. The authority of the Gate of Zion is the authority that the church has today.

Christ is the Gate of Zion; Jesus said, "I am the way." No one can enter Zion except through Jesus; the church is the body of Christ on earth. The church is also the gathering place at the Gate of Zion. The church is the body of Christ, and the church's authority is the authority of Jesus.

> *Verily I say unto you, Whatsoever ye shall bind on earth shall be bound in heaven: and whatsoever ye shall loose on earth shall be loosed in heaven. Again I say unto you, That if two of you shall agree on earth as touching anything that they shall ask, it shall be done for them of my Father which is in heaven. For where two or three are gathered together in my name, there am I in the midst of them. (Mat 18:18-20)*

The church is part of the body of Christ here on earth, with full backing and powers of Christ, who is the Head. Jesus is the Gate of Zion, and the Church is the body of Christ; the church has been given tremendous power to act on behalf of the Head. We are Christ's

Ambassadors and his representatives. Also, the church is referred to as the way (Gate) to salvation Acts 16:17 *"The same followed Paul and us, and cried, saying,* **These men are the servants of the most high God, which shew unto us the way of salvation.**"

Christ will reveal Himself to the world through us, His Body. Through the Church, His Spirit will be made known and operate on Earth.

There were twelve entrances to the city of Jerusalem, and each of these gates had a distinct meaning in the Old Testament. Jesus is now the Gates of the City of Zion, the New Jerusalem. The twelve Gates' functions and spiritual implications have been fulfilled in Christ Jesus. Jesus is the only way to enter Zion, according to the Bible.

The twelve gates represent the scope of the Holy Spirit's activity in the body of Christ.

Jerusalem had twelve entrances, each with a spiritual significance; these gates pointed to everything that Jesus had and is still accomplishing in the Church through the operations of the Holy Spirit.

The kingdom of Christ is physically represented in this world through the Church. Since Jesus is the Head of the Church and the Church is the colony of heaven on Earth, she is endowed with the legislative and judicial authority to act on behalf of the Head.

"And Jesus came and spake unto them, saying, All power is given unto me in heaven and in earth. Go ye therefore…" (Mat. 28:18-19 KJV)

You have been sent to go in the name of Jesus; therefore, you are God's representative here on earth.

> *And I say also unto thee, That thou art Peter, and upon this rock I will build my church; and the gates of hell shall not prevail against it. And I will give unto thee the keys of the kingdom of heaven: and whatsoever thou shalt bind on earth shall be bound in heaven: and whatsoever thou shalt loose on earth shall be loosed in heaven. (Mat 16:18-19).*

The keys to God's kingdom are revealed to and given to the church, which is the pillar of truth and is built upon truth. As a result, the

Church is the only place to go if you want to learn the truth about God. The church is where the Son's truth is made clear. Christ's earthly body, the Church, is where you can learn about the Head.

Christ's authority is carried out through the Church. We represent Him here on Earth. If you persecute the church and try to harm her, you are persecuting Jesus, and Jesus will always respond because that is His body.

People should therefore exercise extreme caution while confronting the church or dealing with issues relating to it.

> *"Saul was breathing out threatening and slaughter against the disciples of the Lord, went to the high priest, And desired of him letters to Damascus to the synagogues, that if he found any of this way, whether they were men or women, he might bring them bound unto Jerusalem. And as he journeyed, he came near Damascus: and suddenly there shined round about him a light from heaven. And he fell to the earth, and heard a voice saying unto him, Saul, Saul, why persecute thou me?" Act 9:1–4 KJV*

"And Paul heard a voice saying unto him, Saul, Saul, why persecute thou me?" Saul was astonished to hear that. He did not know when he was persecuting the church; he did it to Jesus because the church is the body and Bride of Christ. There is no difference between the head and the body.

When Saul was fighting the church in Jerusalem, He was fighting Jesus. He entered every house of believers, and both men and women were imprisoned. Do you know it was Paul who confirmed the death of Stephen? He was there when Stephen was stoned to death. Be careful what you do to the church.

The church is the extension of the kingdom of Zion here on Earth. It is also the gathering of God's chosen people at the Gate of Zion. When the church assembles, anything is possible; it is the gathering of Heaven and Earth.

"By contrast, we have already come near to God in a totally different realm, the Zion-realm, for we have entered the city of the Living God, which is the New Jerusalem in heaven! We have joined the festal gathering of myriads of angels in their joyous celebration! And as members of the church of the Firstborn all our names have been

legally registered as citizens of heaven! And we have come before God who judges all, and who lives among the spirits of the righteous who have been made perfect in his eyes!" (Heb. 12:22-23 TPT)

Power For Change.

Herod fostered persecution of the followers of Jesus during his reign, which was extremely harmful to them. Even the Apostle James was beheaded by him.

King Herod had Peter arrested and imprisoned after realizing how impressed the Jewish authorities were by his choice to persecute Christians. Sixteen soldiers guarded Peter while he was in Herod's care until a public trial could be held.

Peter's freedom was sought after in unceasing prayer. Peter was restrained by two chains the night before he was put on trial; he was lying between two soldiers and surrounded by other guards outside his cell door.

The heartfelt and persistent prayer of the Church (Believer) can accomplish much when put into action and made effective by God. It is dynamic and can have tremendous power.

The Lord's angel appeared at night, and the prison cell was illuminated by heavenly light. To awaken Peter, the angel struck him on the side. The shackles were immediately removed from Peter's wrists. "Wear your clothes and sandals, and follow me," the angel instructed Peter.

Peter hastily walked out of the cell and went after the angel. Peter was miraculously delivered from King Herod. This occurred due to the efforts of believers who understood their role in Zion.

Before reaching the big iron gate that leads to the city, Angel and Peter moved silently past the first guard station and then the second. When they reached the gate, it automatically opened. Peter was delivered from Herod's grasp and what the Jewish authorities had in mind when the Lord sent his angel to intervene.

At the gate of Zion, God's people have gathered in a powerful assembly. Although there was a demonic plot, the Church utilized her power to deliver Peter from the jaws of death.

When put into practice, the sincere and persistent prayer of a good man or group of Believers can achieve much. The early Church knew something we do not yet know today. We would reclaim our towns and neighborhoods for the Lord if we knew.

Believers have refrained from acting by her authority; instead, we quarrel over doctrinal matters while iniquity and evil spread quickly inside our communities. The Church did nothing when King Herod killed James; after learning that it delighted the Jews, Herod again plotted to kill Peter.

When the Gate of hell advanced to seize Peter, the Church rose to fight it off at the Gate of Zion. Herod would have also executed Peter if the congregation had not stood to pray. *Check my book on God Answers Prayer*

The church must fully understand the riches of Christ in us who believes. We are reigning with Christ as His body with authority here on earth. You must fully know what happened from the cross to the throne in His substitutionary Sacrifice. In the Old Testament, these Gats have spiritual interpretation. In this new dispensation, they symbolically point to Christ, His authority, and His ministry today.

The Valley Gate, the Fountain Gate, the Fish Gate, the Old Gate, the Dung Gate, the Water Gate, the Horse Gate, the East Gate, the Gate of Ephraim, the Prison Gate, and the Gate Miphkad, These Gates in the Old Testament, has spiritual connotations, all leads, and point to Jesus. Today these Gates represent Christ and the work that He is doing through the Holy Spirit in the Church, which is His Body.

CHAPTER 6
The Zion Life

Instead, you have come to Mount Zion, to the city of the living God, to the heavenly Jerusalem. You have come to tens of thousands of angels joyfully gathered together and to the assembly of God's firstborn children (whose names are written in heaven). You have come to a judge (the God of all people) and to the spirits of people who have God's approval and have gained eternal life. You have come to Jesus, who brings the new promise from God, and to the sprinkled blood that speaks a better message than Abel's.

(Heb. 12:22-24 GW)

In the New Testament, mount Zion is more of a spiritual kingdom than physical; it is a kingdom with real life, I mean real dwellers. Believers are there now, not later.

*He has rescued us completely from the tyrannical rule of **darkness** **and has translated us into the kingdom realm of his beloved Son.** (Col 1:13 TPT*

That is where we are now; the Bible declared that we are already translated; it is not going to happen; it has happened already. So, you are in Zion now, under the rulership of Christ.

There is a prevailing idea that we must wait until we put off this body in death before we access Zion, all her goodness and splendors. A million times, no! The Zion life starts here on Earth; it will continue after death.

If you have received Jesus, you have the life of God in you, which means you are a citizen of Zion; you have been translated into the kingdom of God.

Eternal life in you is what shows you belong to God. It is your identification Code; on the second coming of Jesus, those who do not have it are not going with Him.

At the second coming of Jesus, only those who have eternal life in their Spirit will be taken. When a believer passes on to the other side of life, it does not mean death but transition; the Bible says such a believer is asleep. There are families in Heaven and on Earth.

For this cause I bow my knees unto the Father of our Lord Jesus Christ, ***Of whom the whole family in heaven and earth is named,*** *(Eph. 3:14-15 KJV).*

You see! We have another family in heaven. This talks about believers who had put off this body in death and transited to Glory.

Eternal life is in your spirit. The body is the limiting factor. It limits the influence of "Zoe" in your body; the more you suppress and mortify your body through the Spirit, the more the life of God in you manifests to your physical body.

But thank God, according to the Gospel of Christ, one day we will put off this mortal body and put on immortality, 1 Corinthians15:53; on that day, death shall be defeated forever, and then we shall live without limitation the fullness of the life of God in us. Hallelujah! This has been the will of the Father from the beginning.

Hallelujah! We rejoice and celebrate the life of God in us. We are already in Zion, in a different realm, while on Earth. We are not of this world. We are Ambassadors of Christ; we live in the Zion realm, hallelujah.

We are not like Moses and the people of Israel; when God visited them on a physical mountain with horrible sight, for them, it was a burning fire with thick clouds of darkness and gloom, Hebrews 12:18 - 21. For us in Christ, it is a place of safety, love, strength, and relationship Hebrew12:22 - 24. Glory to God!

Christ, through His Blood, has ushered us into the city of the Living God, the New Jerusalem! You see! We are here on Earth, but we are operating from the realms and dimensions of Heaven. While on this earth, we live as though in heaven; glory to God!

We have joined the festal gathering of myriads of angels; The city of the living God and heavenly Jerusalem.

Hallelujah! Come on; we are in the city of God now. Enjoy it, live it, and love it. The lives of Zion dwellers are glorious.

You can identify where someone is coming from by the lifestyle he exhibits or how he speaks. Change your attitude and the way you talk. Behave and talk like one who dwells in Zion. Zion dwellers do not talk fear; we do not talk lack and defeat; we talk like our master Jesus.

One day, Lazarus became very sick, almost to death. His sisters informed Jesus that their beloved brother Lazarus was in critical condition. When Jesu heard this, he said, "This sickness will not end in death for Lazarus."

Talk like Jesus; this problem will not end in death; tell yourself you are coming out of that problem stronger, better, and with vitality. Hallelujah!

Whatever you are going through now will end up in praise. Glory to God! This event revealed the greatness of Jesus. The problem you are in now was not brought to you by God, but God will reveal His Power in your life through it. Hallelujah!

Despite his love for Mary, Martha, and Lazarus, Jesus stayed in the same place for two more days. He finally revealed to his Apostles on the third day. "Lazarus, our friend, has just fallen asleep. It's time that I go and awaken him." Jesus did not say it the way it was. He said what he wanted to see, for Jesus said that "Lazarus was not dead but sleeping, "so He was going to wake him up from sleep.

Lazarus had already been in the tomb for four days. Do not complain as Mather did. Zion dwellers do not complain; we do not murmur; yes, we do not! Mather! Who told you that Jesus was late? God cannot be late for anything.

Mather said, "Lord, if only you had been here, my brother would not have died." Refuse the spirit of complaining and grumbling. Mather is now blaming Jesus for her brother's death.

This man died and was in the grave for four days, and Jesus said Lazarus was sleeping. This is faith in action. Jesus asked, "Where did you bury him?" People must have been asking why Jesus did not come in time. But you know, Jesus is never late. Glory to God!

Jesus told them, "Roll away the stone." With a loud voice, Jesus shouted with authority, "Lazarus! Come out of the tomb!" Lazarus came forth, hallelujah. Jesus did not express or talk about fear at the grave of Lazarus. He was strong in faith, only saying what he wanted to see.

I remember bringing a domestic worker into my house; we took time to teach her how things work in our house, and for the first month, it was teaching. Every Christian should do this when they arrive in Zion - when they become born again.

When you are born again, try as much as possible to learn how things are done in Zion; attitude and mindset are very important. Take time, and learn how-to live-in Zion.

Imagine Paul and Silas in prison; they were beaten, and their legs were in stock. This guy knew how to operate with the wisdom of Zion; they started worshipping God and singing praise in that condition. For some people, it will be a time to complain and blame God for allowing such things to happen to them. But they understood how the Kingdom works.

Every tourist must have a handbook concerning the country he is visiting and a tour guide to navigate around. Just imagine tourists without maps and GPS; you will find it difficult to find your way around that city.

I thank God for the Holy Spirit; you will never go wrong if you can listen to Him. The Holy Spirit will always lead you in the right direction and teach you everything.

The Love Life

In Zion, love is the way of life; everything exists through love. Love brings you into the frequency of God, for love is light; as far as you walk in it, you walk under the floodlight of heaven, and you will never stumble.

Believers who are supposed to walk in the light are already stumbling as though they are in darkness; it should not be, so any time you walk away from love, you are walking away from the floodlight of heaven.

Imagine what life would be like when you walked away from light. What happens is that darkness takes over.

Sometimes we wonder why so and so Christian could do such and such despite being a leader in the Church; it is because he momentarily left the light and stumbled into the dark path, and Satan takes that opportunity to wreak havoc.

Do not walk away from the love the Holy Ghost has implanted in you since your salvation.

The nature of God in you is love, and it is for your good. It is for your smooth sailing as a believer. Can you picture a sailor who does not have a compass or a beautiful automobile without an engine? That is a believer without operating in love. Faith goes hand in hand with love. Show me a man with strong faith, and I will show you a man who walks in love.

Do you see why some Believers' faith is not producing results? It is not that you do not have faith; your lack of love has rendered your faith impotent.

Your heartbeat should always be to love everyone that comes your way. While going into Ministry, I advised myself to love everyone without partiality and never play a role that would cause love to flee.

Despise hate and embrace everything good and virtuous; tenderly love your fellow Zion dwellers as members of one family.

ABOUT THE BOOK

Though we are in the world, we are not of it; our Citizenship is in Heaven; therefore, believers operate from the Spiritual dimension where Christ rules as King. Believers are in the kingdom of Christ now, not in the sweet by and by. Eternal life starts here on Earth; this life is What you received when you said Yes to Jesus; when you become aware that the very life of God is in you, the knowledge will stir you up to take hold of the things that belong to you as a citizen of Heaven. Healing belongs to you; prosperity is yours. You're a child of God, hence joint heir with Christ. The same Spirit that raised Christ from the dead is in you. Therefore, you cannot fail.

ABOUT THE AUTHOR

Charles Paul is a missionary and the coordinator of All Youths for Christ. He is an anointed teacher and preacher of God's word, called with the mandate of reaching out to the world with the gospel of our Lord Jesus Christ. He is happily married with a blessed family.

Made in the USA
Middletown, DE
21 September 2023